EMMANUEL JOSEPH

The Intentional Hour, Crafting Daily Moments of Focus, Calm, and Connection

Copyright © 2025 by Emmanuel Joseph

All rights reserved. No part of this publication may be reproduced, stored or transmitted in any form or by any means, electronic, mechanical, photocopying, recording, scanning, or otherwise without written permission from the publisher. It is illegal to copy this book, post it to a website, or distribute it by any other means without permission.

First edition

This book was professionally typeset on Reedsy.
Find out more at reedsy.com

Contents

1	Chapter 1: Embracing the Intentional Hour	1
2	Chapter 2: The Power of Morning Rituals	3
3	Chapter 3: Anchoring in Mindfulness	5
4	Chapter 4: The Art of Self-Reflection	7
5	Chapter 5: Cultivating Gratitude	9
6	Chapter 6: The Role of Nature in Nurturing Calm	10
7	Chapter 7: Digital Detox	12
8	Chapter 8: The Magic of Creative Expression	13
9	Chapter 9: Nourishing the Body	15
10	Chapter 10: Building Meaningful Connections	17
11	Chapter 11: The Practice of Acceptance	19
12	Chapter 12: Setting Intentions and Goals	21
13	Chapter 13: The Healing Power of Rest	23
14	Chapter 14: The Joy of Learning	24
15	Chapter 15: Acts of Kindness	26
16	Chapter 16: Embracing Change	28
17	Chapter 17: Crafting Your Intentional Hour	30

1

Chapter 1: Embracing the Intentional Hour

In a world that races against time, finding a moment to breathe and reflect can feel like a luxury. Yet, the value of setting aside an intentional hour for oneself can be transformative. This chapter introduces the concept of the intentional hour, emphasizing its importance in nurturing focus, calm, and connection. By being deliberate in our actions and thoughts, we can create a sanctuary of serenity amidst the chaos of daily life. Imagine an hour where the outside world fades, and you immerse yourself in what truly matters.

The intentional hour is not about perfection but presence. It's about carving out a dedicated time each day to reconnect with yourself and your surroundings. In this hour, you allow yourself to slow down, breathe deeply, and savor the beauty of the moment. This practice fosters a sense of inner peace and clarity that permeates the rest of the day. By prioritizing this hour, you signal to yourself that your well-being matters.

Creating an intentional hour begins with setting an intention. What do you hope to achieve or experience during this time? Whether it's a moment of quiet reflection, a burst of creative inspiration, or a sense of calm, having a clear intention helps guide your actions. This hour becomes a canvas where you paint your desires, dreams, and aspirations. It's a space where you can be fully present, fully yourself.

As you embark on this journey of intentionality, remember that it's a practice, not a destination. There will be days when the hour feels effortless and days when distractions creep in. Embrace both with grace and patience. The intentional hour is a gift you give yourself, a promise to honor your needs and desires. It's a commitment to living life with purpose and mindfulness.

2

Chapter 2: The Power of Morning Rituals

Morning rituals set the tone for the day. This chapter explores how dedicating the first hour after waking to mindful practices can elevate your entire day. From gentle stretches to gratitude journaling, incorporating purposeful activities into your morning routine can infuse your day with energy and clarity. The dawn of a new day offers a blank canvas; painting it with intention creates a masterpiece of focused productivity and serene calm.

A well-crafted morning ritual can be as simple or as elaborate as you desire. Some may find solace in a quiet cup of tea, while others may thrive on a morning workout. The key is to choose activities that resonate with you and set a positive tone for the day ahead. By beginning your day with intention, you create a foundation of stability and purpose.

Consistency is crucial when establishing morning rituals. It may take time to find the perfect combination of activities that work for you, but the effort is worth it. Over time, these rituals become second nature, providing a sense of structure and comfort. Morning rituals are a gift to yourself, a way to honor the start of a new day with mindfulness and intention.

As you experiment with different practices, remember to be kind to yourself. Some days may not go as planned, and that's okay. The beauty of morning rituals lies in their flexibility and adaptability. They are not about perfection but about creating a moment of intentionality that aligns with your needs and aspirations.

3

Chapter 3: Anchoring in Mindfulness

Mindfulness is the art of being present. This chapter delves into practical techniques to anchor oneself in the present moment during the intentional hour. Through mindful breathing exercises, body scans, and meditation practices, readers learn to cultivate a sense of calm and awareness. In a world filled with distractions, mastering mindfulness becomes a powerful tool to navigate life's ebbs and flows with grace.

Mindful breathing is a simple yet profound practice. By focusing on the breath, you can bring your attention to the present moment and create a sense of inner calm. Start by finding a comfortable seated position and take a few deep breaths. Notice the sensation of the breath as it enters and leaves your body. If your mind starts to wander, gently guide it back to the breath. This practice can be done anywhere and anytime, making it a versatile tool for cultivating mindfulness.

Body scans are another effective technique for anchoring in the present moment. Begin by lying down or sitting comfortably. Close your eyes and take a few deep breaths to relax. Slowly bring your attention to different parts of your body, starting from your toes and moving up to your head. Notice any sensations, tension, or areas of relaxation. This practice helps you tune into your body's signals and fosters a deeper connection with yourself.

Meditation is a cornerstone of mindfulness practice. Set aside a few minutes

THE INTENTIONAL HOUR, CRAFTING DAILY MOMENTS OF FOCUS, CALM, AND CONNECTION

each day to sit in stillness and observe your thoughts without judgment. Focus on your breath or use a guided meditation to help you stay present. Over time, meditation can enhance your ability to remain calm and centered amidst life's challenges. The intentional hour becomes a sanctuary for mindfulness, a time to cultivate awareness and presence.

4

Chapter 4: The Art of Self-Reflection

Self-reflection is a journey inward. This chapter guides readers through the process of introspection during the intentional hour. By asking meaningful questions and engaging in honest self-assessment, individuals gain insights into their thoughts, emotions, and actions. Journaling prompts and reflective exercises are provided to facilitate this deep dive into one's inner world. The intentional hour becomes a sacred space for personal growth and self-discovery.

Journaling is a powerful tool for self-reflection. Start by setting aside a few minutes each day to write about your thoughts and experiences. Use prompts such as "What am I grateful for today?" or "What challenges did I face and how did I overcome them?" to guide your reflections. Writing allows you to process your emotions and gain clarity on your life's direction.

Another effective practice is to ask yourself meaningful questions. Consider questions like "What are my core values?" or "What brings me joy?" Take time to ponder these questions and write down your answers. This process helps you uncover your true desires and align your actions with your values. Self-reflection is an ongoing journey, and these questions can evolve as you grow and change.

Engaging in self-assessment can also provide valuable insights. Take stock of your achievements, challenges, and areas for improvement. Celebrate your successes and identify opportunities for growth. This practice fosters a sense of accountability and empowers you to take proactive steps toward personal development.

5

Chapter 5: Cultivating Gratitude

Gratitude is a potent antidote to negativity. This chapter emphasizes the transformative power of gratitude during the intentional hour. Through practices such as gratitude lists, letters, and visualization, readers learn to shift their focus from what they lack to what they have. By consistently acknowledging the blessings in their lives, individuals foster a positive mindset and a deeper sense of contentment.

Creating a gratitude list is a simple yet powerful practice. Set aside a few minutes each day to write down things you're grateful for. They can be as grand as a loving family or as simple as a warm cup of coffee in the morning. The act of writing helps solidify these positive thoughts and can serve as a reminder of the abundance in your life.

Gratitude letters are another impactful exercise. Think of someone who has made a significant positive impact on your life and write them a heartfelt letter expressing your appreciation. You don't have to send the letter if you prefer not to, but the act of writing allows you to reflect on the positive influence they've had on you. This exercise not only cultivates gratitude but also strengthens your sense of connection.

Visualization is a powerful technique for embodying gratitude. Take a few minutes to close your eyes and visualize moments or people you're grateful for. Imagine the feelings of joy, love, and appreciation as vividly as possible. This practice can elevate your mood and create a sense of peace and fulfillment.

6

Chapter 6: The Role of Nature in Nurturing Calm

Nature has an innate ability to soothe and inspire. This chapter explores how incorporating nature into the intentional hour can enhance feelings of tranquility and connection. Whether through a walk in the park, gardening, or simply sitting by a window, engaging with the natural world provides a respite from the digital realm. Nature's beauty and rhythms remind us of the interconnectedness of all life and our place within it.

Taking a walk in nature is a simple yet profound way to reconnect with the natural world. Find a park, forest, or any green space and take a leisurely stroll. Pay attention to the sights, sounds, and smells around you. Notice the rustling leaves, the chirping birds, and the gentle breeze. This mindful walk can ground you in the present moment and provide a sense of calm and clarity.

Gardening is another wonderful way to engage with nature. Whether you have a sprawling garden or a few potted plants, tending to plants can be a meditative and rewarding activity. The act of nurturing and watching plants grow fosters a sense of connection and responsibility. Gardening also provides an opportunity to observe the cycles of nature and appreciate the beauty of life.

CHAPTER 6: THE ROLE OF NATURE IN NURTURING CALM

If outdoor activities are not possible, simply sitting by a window and observing nature can be equally soothing. Find a comfortable spot by a window and take a few moments to watch the sky, the trees, or the birds. This practice allows you to pause and appreciate the natural world, even from indoors. The intentional hour becomes a time to immerse yourself in nature's calming presence.

7

Chapter 7: Digital Detox

In an era of constant connectivity, a digital detox becomes essential. This chapter discusses the benefits of disconnecting from screens during the intentional hour. By limiting exposure to digital devices, individuals create space for meaningful activities and authentic interactions. Practical tips for setting boundaries with technology are shared, empowering readers to reclaim their time and attention.

Setting boundaries with technology starts with creating designated screen-free zones and times. For example, make your bedroom a no-screen zone or establish an hour before bedtime as screen-free time. This helps reduce the constant bombardment of digital stimuli and creates a conducive environment for relaxation and rest.

Another effective strategy is to turn off notifications and set specific times for checking emails and social media. Constant notifications can be distracting and disruptive, making it challenging to stay present. By setting designated times to check your devices, you can be more intentional with your digital interactions and reduce mindless scrolling.

Engage in activities that don't require screens during the intentional hour. Read a book, take a walk, meditate, or spend time with loved ones. These activities provide a refreshing break from the digital world and allow you to connect with yourself and others in meaningful ways. The intentional hour becomes a time to unplug and recharge.

8

Chapter 8: The Magic of Creative Expression

Creativity is a conduit for self-expression. This chapter explores how engaging in creative activities during the intentional hour can unlock new perspectives and emotional release. Whether through painting, writing, or playing an instrument, readers are encouraged to explore their creative passions. The intentional hour becomes a playground for imagination, where self-doubt gives way to artistic exploration.

Painting is a wonderful way to express your emotions and ideas. Whether you're an experienced artist or a beginner, the act of putting brush to canvas can be incredibly liberating. Use this time to experiment with colors, shapes, and textures. Allow yourself to create without judgment or the need for perfection. The process of painting can be therapeutic and provide a sense of accomplishment.

Writing is another powerful form of creative expression. Set aside time to write freely, whether it's journaling, poetry, or storytelling. Writing allows you to articulate your thoughts and emotions, providing clarity and release. Don't worry about grammar or structure; focus on letting your words flow naturally. The intentional hour becomes a sanctuary for your inner voice.

Playing a musical instrument can also be a deeply fulfilling creative activity. Whether you're strumming a guitar, playing the piano, or experimenting with percussion, music allows you to connect with your emotions and express yourself in a unique way. The intentional hour becomes a time to explore melodies and rhythms, creating a harmonious space for creativity.

9

Chapter 9: Nourishing the Body

P hysical well-being is integral to overall balance. This chapter highlights the importance of nourishing the body during the intentional hour. From mindful eating to gentle exercise, readers learn to tune into their physical needs and prioritize self-care. Recipes and movement routines are provided to inspire a holistic approach to wellness. The intentional hour becomes a time to honor and nurture the body's wisdom.

Mindful eating is a practice of paying full attention to the experience of eating and drinking. During the intentional hour, prepare a meal or snack with care and focus on the process of eating. Notice the colors, textures, and flavors of the food. Chew slowly and savor each bite. This practice not only enhances the enjoyment of food but also promotes better digestion and a deeper connection with your body's needs.

Gentle exercise, such as yoga, tai chi, or stretching, can also be incorporated into the intentional hour. These activities promote flexibility, strength, and relaxation. Follow a guided routine or create your own sequence of movements. Focus on your breath and the sensations in your body as you move. This mindful approach to exercise helps reduce stress and enhances overall well-being.

Hydration is another essential aspect of nourishing the body. During the intentional hour, make it a habit to drink a glass of water or herbal tea. Staying hydrated supports optimal bodily functions and boosts energy levels. Use this time to reflect on how you can incorporate more hydration into your daily routine.

10

Chapter 10: Building Meaningful Connections

Human connections enrich our lives. This chapter emphasizes the value of fostering meaningful relationships during the intentional hour. Through acts of kindness, heartfelt conversations, and quality time with loved ones, readers strengthen their bonds with others. Tips for deepening connections and cultivating empathy are shared, reminding readers that intentional interactions build a supportive community.

Acts of kindness can be as simple as writing a thank-you note, offering a compliment, or helping a neighbor. These small gestures create a ripple effect of positivity and strengthen connections with others. During the intentional hour, find opportunities to perform acts of kindness and observe how they impact both you and the recipient.

Heartfelt conversations are a cornerstone of meaningful relationships. Set aside time during the intentional hour to engage in deep and meaningful conversations with loved ones. Listen actively and share your thoughts and feelings openly. This practice fosters trust and intimacy, creating a strong foundation for lasting relationships.

Quality time with loved ones can take many forms, from shared meals to outdoor activities. Plan activities that allow you to connect and create lasting memories. Whether it's a game night, a hike, or a simple walk in the park, these moments of togetherness strengthen the bonds of friendship and family. The intentional hour becomes a time to nurture and cherish your relationships.

11

Chapter 11: The Practice of Acceptance

Acceptance is a key component of inner peace. This chapter delves into the practice of accepting oneself and one's circumstances during the intentional hour. Through exercises in self-compassion and radical acceptance, readers learn to embrace their imperfections and navigate challenges with resilience. The intentional hour becomes a sanctuary for self-acceptance and emotional healing.

Self-compassion involves treating yourself with the same kindness and understanding that you would offer to a friend. During the intentional hour, practice self-compassion by acknowledging your struggles and offering yourself words of comfort and encouragement. Remember that everyone makes mistakes and faces challenges; it's a natural part of being human.

Radical acceptance is the practice of accepting reality as it is, without trying to change or resist it. This doesn't mean giving up or condoning harmful situations, but rather acknowledging what is beyond your control. During the intentional hour, reflect on areas of your life where you struggle with acceptance. Practice letting go of resistance and embracing reality with an open heart.

Mindful self-reflection is another powerful tool for cultivating acceptance. Take time during the intentional hour to reflect on your thoughts and emotions without judgment. Observe your inner experiences with curiosity and understanding. This practice helps you develop a deeper sense of self-awareness and acceptance.

12

Chapter 12: Setting Intentions and Goals

Intentions and goals provide direction and purpose. This chapter guides readers in setting meaningful intentions and achievable goals during the intentional hour. By aligning their actions with their values and aspirations, individuals create a roadmap for personal and professional growth. Strategies for effective goal-setting and visualization are shared, empowering readers to manifest their dreams.

Setting intentions is about clarifying what you want to achieve or experience. During the intentional hour, take a few moments to reflect on your values and priorities. What matters most to you? What do you hope to accomplish? Write down your intentions and keep them in a place where you can revisit them regularly. These intentions serve as a guiding light for your actions and decisions.

Goal-setting involves breaking down your intentions into specific, measurable, and achievable steps. Use the SMART criteria (Specific, Measurable, Achievable, Relevant, Time-bound) to create clear and actionable goals. During the intentional hour, identify one or two goals you want to focus on and create a plan to achieve them. Break your goals into smaller tasks and set deadlines to keep yourself on track.

Visualization is a powerful technique for manifesting your goals. During the intentional hour, take a few minutes to visualize yourself achieving your goals. Imagine the details of your success, including how it feels and what it looks like. This mental rehearsal helps reinforce your commitment and motivates you to take action.

13

Chapter 13: The Healing Power of Rest

Rest is essential for rejuvenation. This chapter underscores the importance of incorporating rest into the intentional hour. From power naps to relaxation techniques, readers learn to prioritize downtime as a vital aspect of self-care. The intentional hour becomes a time to recharge and replenish, fostering resilience and well-being.

Power naps can be incredibly revitalizing. A short nap of 10-20 minutes can boost alertness and improve mood. Find a quiet, comfortable spot, set an alarm, and allow yourself to drift into a light sleep. This brief rest can provide the energy and focus needed to tackle the rest of the day with vigor.

Relaxation techniques such as deep breathing, progressive muscle relaxation, and guided imagery can also be beneficial. During the intentional hour, practice these techniques to release tension and promote a sense of calm. Deep breathing involves taking slow, deep breaths to activate the body's relaxation response. Progressive muscle relaxation involves tensing and then relaxing each muscle group in the body, promoting overall relaxation. Guided imagery involves visualizing calming and peaceful scenes to reduce stress and enhance well-being.

Creating a restful environment is also important. Ensure that your space is comfortable, quiet, and free from distractions. Use soft lighting, soothing sounds, and comfortable furnishings to create a peaceful atmosphere. The intentional hour becomes a sanctuary for rest and rejuvenation.

14

Chapter 14: The Joy of Learning

Learning is a lifelong adventure. This chapter explores how dedicating the intentional hour to learning new skills and acquiring knowledge can stimulate the mind and spark curiosity. Whether through reading, online courses, or exploring new hobbies, readers are encouraged to embrace the joy of continuous learning. The intentional hour becomes a gateway to intellectual growth and personal enrichment.

Reading is a wonderful way to expand your knowledge and stimulate your mind. Choose books, articles, or journals that interest you and set aside time during the intentional hour to read. Whether it's fiction, non-fiction, or poetry, reading can open up new worlds and perspectives. Make a list of books you want to read and enjoy the process of discovering new ideas and insights.

Online courses and tutorials are also excellent resources for learning. Explore platforms that offer courses in subjects you're passionate about, whether it's photography, coding, or cooking. Dedicate time during the intentional hour to watch videos, complete assignments, and practice new skills. This structured approach to learning can enhance your expertise and provide a sense of accomplishment.

Exploring new hobbies is another way to embrace the joy of learning. Whether it's painting, gardening, or playing a musical instrument, trying new activities can ignite creativity and curiosity. During the intentional hour, set

CHAPTER 14: THE JOY OF LEARNING

aside time to experiment with new hobbies and enjoy the process of learning and growing. The intentional hour becomes a time to nurture your passions and discover new talents.

15

Chapter 15: Acts of Kindness

Kindness is a ripple that creates waves of positivity. This chapter highlights the impact of performing acts of kindness during the intentional hour. From volunteering to simple gestures of compassion, readers learn to infuse their lives with generosity and goodwill. The intentional hour becomes a platform for spreading kindness and making a difference in the world.

Volunteering is a powerful way to give back to the community. During the intentional hour, find opportunities to volunteer for causes you're passionate about. Whether it's helping at a local shelter, participating in community clean-ups, or mentoring others, volunteering can create a sense of purpose and fulfillment. The act of giving your time and energy to others can have a profound impact on both you and those you help.

Simple gestures of compassion, such as offering a listening ear, providing assistance, or sending a thoughtful message, can also make a significant difference. During the intentional hour, look for opportunities to extend kindness to those around you. These small acts create a ripple effect, spreading positivity and connection.

Practicing random acts of kindness can also be rewarding. Pay for someone's coffee, leave a kind note for a colleague, or donate to a charity. These spontaneous acts of generosity can brighten someone's day and remind you of the power of kindness. The intentional hour becomes a time to spread

CHAPTER 15: ACTS OF KINDNESS

joy and compassion in the world.

16

Chapter 16: Embracing Change

Change is a constant in life. This chapter addresses the process of navigating change with grace and adaptability during the intentional hour. Through practices of mindfulness and resilience-building, readers learn to embrace uncertainty and transform challenges into opportunities. The intentional hour becomes a time to cultivate a growth mindset and thrive amidst change.

Mindfulness practices, such as meditation and deep breathing, can help you stay grounded during times of change. During the intentional hour, use these techniques to center yourself and remain present. Mindfulness allows you to observe your thoughts and emotions without judgment, providing clarity and calm in the face of uncertainty.

Resilience-building involves developing the skills and mindset needed to navigate challenges. Reflect on past experiences where you successfully adapted to change and identify the strengths and strategies you used. During the intentional hour, practice resilience-building activities such as journaling, visualization, and goal-setting. These practices help you develop a positive outlook and the confidence to face change with courage.

Embracing a growth mindset is also essential for thriving amidst change. View challenges as opportunities for learning and growth. During the intentional hour, set intentions to approach change with curiosity and openness. Celebrate your progress and acknowledge your efforts, even if the outcome is not as expected. The intentional hour becomes a time to cultivate resilience and embrace the journey of change.

17

Chapter 17: Crafting Your Intentional Hour

In the final chapter, readers are guided to design their unique intentional hour. By integrating the practices and insights from previous chapters, individuals create a personalized blueprint for daily moments of focus, calm, and connection. Practical tips for maintaining consistency and flexibility are shared, ensuring that the intentional hour becomes a cherished and sustainable part of their lives.

Begin by reflecting on the practices that resonate most with you. What activities bring you joy, peace, and a sense of fulfillment? Create a list of these practices and consider how you can incorporate them into your intentional hour. Remember that the intentional hour is a flexible and evolving practice, so feel free to experiment and adjust as needed.

Set a regular time for your intentional hour and create a routine that works for your lifestyle. Whether it's in the morning, afternoon, or evening, consistency is key. Communicate your commitment to others and set boundaries to protect this sacred time. Consider using a planner or journal to track your intentional hour activities and reflect on your progress.

Flexibility is also important. Life can be unpredictable, and there may be days when your routine is disrupted. Allow yourself to adapt and be kind to yourself if things don't go as planned. The intentional hour is not about rigid

CHAPTER 17: CRAFTING YOUR INTENTIONAL HOUR

rules but about creating a space for self-care and mindfulness.

Celebrate your intentional hour by acknowledging the positive impact it has on your life. Reflect on the moments of focus, calm, and connection you've experienced. Share your journey with others and inspire them to create their own intentional hour. The intentional hour becomes a cherished and sustainable practice that enriches your life.

The Intentional Hour: Crafting Daily Moments of Focus, Calm, and Connection

In a fast-paced world where moments of true connection and calm seem fleeting, "The Intentional Hour" offers a transformative guide to reclaiming your day. This insightful book invites you to carve out an hour each day dedicated to focus, mindfulness, and meaningful interactions. Through practical techniques and heartwarming anecdotes, you'll discover how to create a sanctuary of serenity amidst life's chaos.

From the power of morning rituals to the magic of creative expression, each chapter provides actionable steps to nurture your mind, body, and soul. Whether it's through mindfulness practices, self-reflection, or acts of kindness, "The Intentional Hour" empowers you to live with intention and purpose. Embrace the journey of crafting daily moments that bring joy, clarity, and connection into your life.

With its gentle guidance and inspiring insights, "The Intentional Hour" is a beacon for anyone seeking to cultivate a balanced and fulfilling life. Join the movement of intentional living and transform your ordinary hours into extraordinary moments of growth and serenity.

www.ingramcontent.com/pod-product-compliance
Lightning Source LLC
LaVergne TN
LVHW020739090526
838202LV00057BA/6124